Create Your Life:

An intention-setting workbook

make your perfect

Create Your Life: An Intention-Setting Workbook
This book was designed by Gaby Merediz, life coach and mentor at: Make Your Perfect, part of Tmuffin™

Follow Make Your Perfect at http://makeyourperfect.com

Copyright © 2017 Tmuffin™
All rights reserved. May not be replicated or reproduced without written permission from Tmuffin™.

Show us your perfect.

You are an artist.
Share your masterpieces with the world.

@makeyourperfect   facebook.com/   @makeyourperfect
                     makeyourperfect

Want to join a secret society of women making their version of perfect?

Join Today

become part of it at http://makeyourperfect.com/powerhouse

About This Book

Setting intentions is so important to achieving the life that you want. Intentions create your life. We are so stuck on society's definition of productivity and success that we often feel the need to create a final product. We forget that even setting intentions is an act of creation. Where your thoughts go, life will flow.

Intentions help you focus your thoughts, manifest what you want, and have the experiences that you want to have.

You are the creator of your life. You set the rules. Start by setting your intentions.

I have historically had trouble setting intentions. I might read something really inspiring, set a grand intention, and feel like a failure when my intention doesn't materialize. Or else I go to the other end of the spectrum and am so stuck by the little voices in my head ranting about my limiting beliefs that I don't really set the intentions that uplevel my energy and my life.

Plus, I get so bogged down in all of the thoughts going through my brain that I worry that I'm going to forget something important when I'm setting intentions.

I created this book to help myself set intentions, and it has worked so well that I had to share. Go to http://makeyourperfect.com/intention-setting-stories to read about some of my personal experiences with intention setting.

Here's to making some magic and creating the life that you want.

Mwa,

Gaby

How To Use This Book:

This book repeats the same 4 pages over and over. You can use each 5-page bundle to work on setting one intention for a certain time period. However, you can always go back and revisit what you've written if you need inspiration for setting future intentions.

Page 1: Intention Brainstorm

Put your pen on the paper, and start writing. Stop judging yourself, and spit out some train-of-thought ideas. As you reach each prompt, see if you can really go with it. By the time you reach the "refine it" prompt, you can go back and circle, highlight or underline the ideas that stood out to you. See if you can put them together into a sentence or short paragraph.

Page 2: I Will...

This is where you can play with your feelings of excitement and come face to face with limiting beliefs. Notice what feelings come up when you write what you're excited about. Check with yourself to see if you feel any release when you jot down your fears surrounding this intention.

Page 3: Feel It

This page takes your intention a little further. You focus on how you feel when you're living with the intention, and you use your imagination, which is really the channel to your higher self and other frequencies. You can get as deep and creative with this step as you want, or you can skip it altogether. It would be interesting to note how your intention materializes when you do this step, though.

Page 4: Indulgence

Page 4 asks you what you can indulge in to support this intention. Bringing all of your senses into your intention setting can help you connect with the physical world as well as the energy within and around you. Consider whether you can do something to indulge your senses of sight, hearing, taste, smell and touch in a way that's blissful. When you're turned on by your intention, you're much more likely to focus on it and allow it to materialize.

Page 5: Reflect

It's always a good idea to make notes of the magic that happens in your life. Use this page to increase your awareness, practice gratitude and reward yourself for taking part in this experiment as you explore your journey.

FAQs — (Go to makeyourperfect.com/intention-faqs for more.)

Is an intention the same as a goal or a mission?

An intention is similar to a goal or a mission. It sets the tone for your actions, for the life you want to create. I like to think of an intention as a declaration of your will instead of something that has a specific final outcome. However, it can be whatever works for you.

What should an intention look like?

An intention is a declaration of will. It can look like whatever you want. Part of the work that you'll do in this book involves brainstorming your ideas so that you can pull out what you need to create an intention.

Some examples of an intention are:

- I will listen and observe instead of analyze and judge.
- I will move my body for 10 minutes a day for the next 10 days.
- I will embody the persona of a powerful, confident woman.

Should I set big visions or smaller intentions?

An intention can be as short, simple, vague, detailed or complex as you need it to be. You may find that using the book to set a big vision is helpful. Then, you can break that down into smaller, baby-step intentions. It's totally up to you.

Should I approach intention setting in a specific way?

I love rituals. They can help you create sacred space and tap into the energy that goes beyond this physical realm.

You may want to take a deep breath, go to a quiet room, and light a candle before working in this book. However, you can also carry it with you and pull it out at the train station or hide in the bathroom as your kids watch TV and get some thoughts out. This is meant to take the overwhelming ideas and energy that pervade your busy life and harness them into something clear and meaningful, whether you have a minute to yourself or not really.

Why do I have to keep repeating my intention on more than one page?

Part of believing in your intention involves internalizing it. The more you repeat it, the better you will be able to internalize it.

What if my intention doesn't "come true"?

An intention is more like a guideline for your actions than a prediction of the future. Setting an intention and really focusing on it puts out a certain vibration. Because like attracts like, you will manifest reactions from the universe that have a similar vibration.

If you set a really lofty intention from the get-go, your rational mind might be sending judgments, negativity and fears that block you from really focusing on it and taking intentional action.

Try starting with baby steps. The more you keep the promises that you set for yourself and others, the stronger your will becomes, and the better you get at escaping that monkey mind that tells you that you'll never get what you want.

Page 2 helps you work through your fears, or limiting beliefs, so that you can become aware of them as you take action on your intention.

What is the point of setting an intention?

Setting intentions helps you create and cultivate your life. If you're feeling stuck or stagnant, that creation vibration creates movement that allows you to steer. If you're already moving forward, intentions can help clarify your paths and experiences.

In the simplest terms, intention setting can help you show up for life. And when you show up, you better connect with the world. And when you're living with connections to yourself, others and the universe, you thrive.

Also, the manner in which you show up in one facet of your life is the same way that you show up in other facets in your life. Showing up to your intentions gives you permission to start showing up authentically everywhere, and that's when the magic happens.

Intention Brainstorm

OK, just start writing. "I intend to..."

STOP. What do I want to bring into my life?

HOLD ON. Breathe. Close your eyes. Picture it. What does your heart desire?

Refine it. Put it all together.

Write it here. My intention is:

I will:

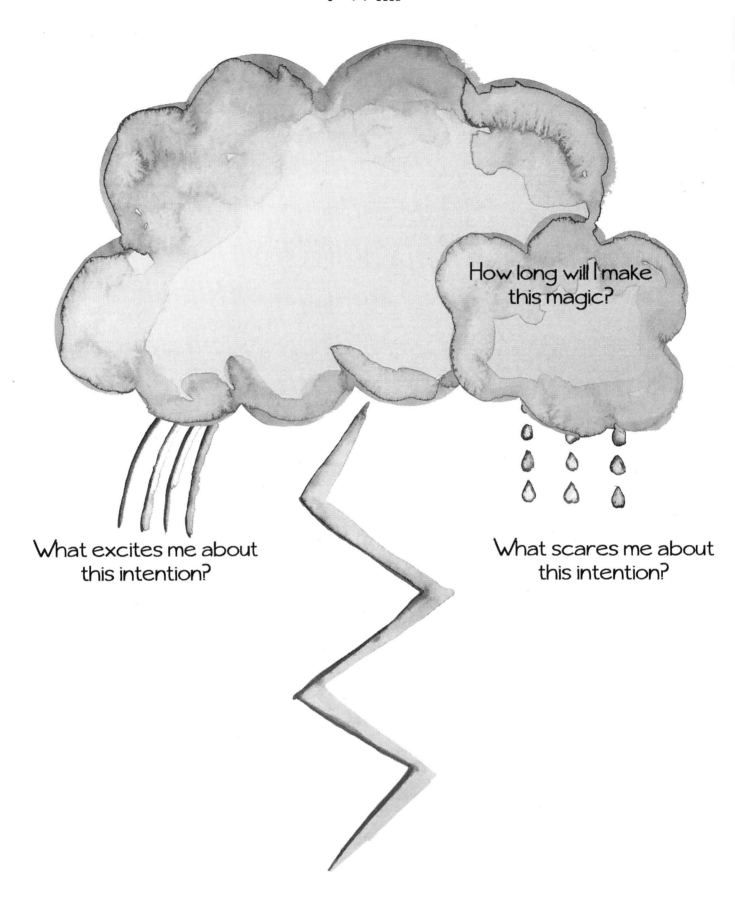

How long will I make this magic?

What excites me about this intention?

What scares me about this intention?

Feel It

Sink into the embodiment of who you will be, what you will feel and what your life will be like when your intention materializes. If you're up for it, write a fable, make a doodle, draw a picture or even just scribble with a color that represents this.

Indulge

Rewrite your intention above.
What can you indulge in that supports your intention?

Reflect

The more you notice the magic that happens, the more it will happen. Use this page to keep track of synchronicities throughout your intention period, write down things for which you're grateful, and reward yourself for loving yourself or taking action. Come back to this page frequently, and watch how the magic unfolds.

Intention Brainstorm

OK, just start writing. "I intend to..."

STOP. What do I want to bring into my life?

HOLD ON. Breathe. Close your eyes. Picture it. What does your heart desire?

Refine it. Put it all together.

Write it here. My intention is:

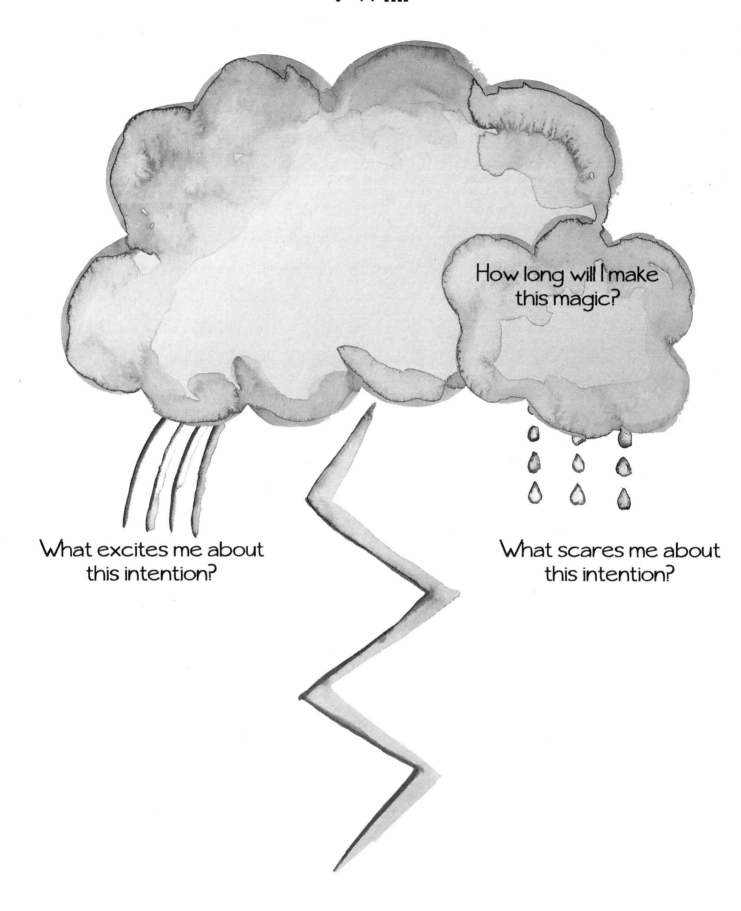

Feel It

Sink into the embodiment of who you will be, what you will feel and what your life will be like when your intention materializes. If you're up for it, write a fable, make a doodle, draw a picture or even just scribble with a color that represents this.

Indulge

Rewrite your intention above.
What can you indulge in that supports your intention?

Reflect

The more you notice the magic that happens, the more it will happen. Use this page to keep track of synchronicities throughout your intention period, write down things for which you're grateful, and reward yourself for loving yourself or taking action. Come back to this page frequently, and watch how the magic unfolds.

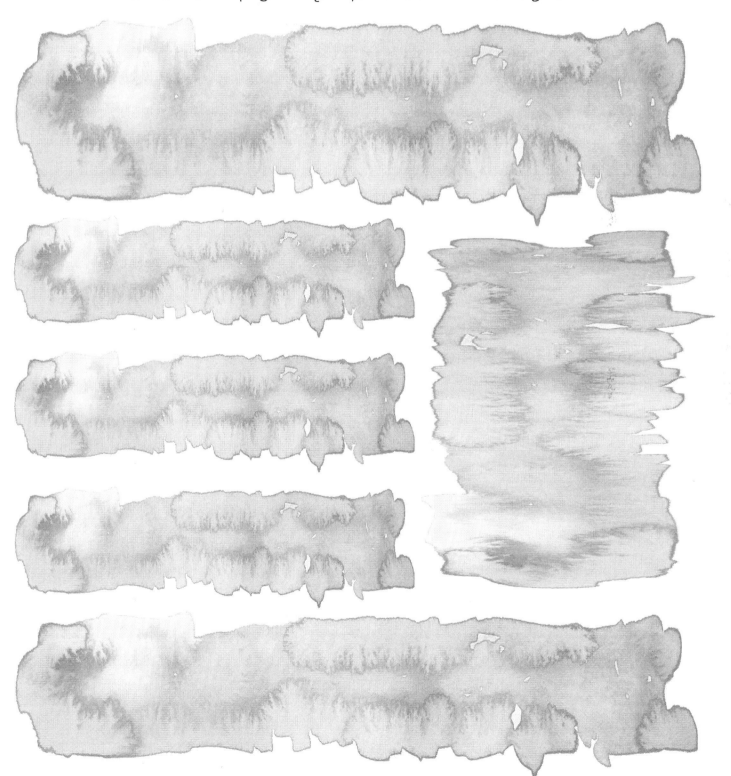

Intention Brainstorm

OK, just start writing. "I intend to..."

STOP. What do I want to bring into my life?

HOLD ON. Breathe. Close your eyes. Picture it. What does your heart desire?

Refine it. Put it all together.

Write it here. My intention is:

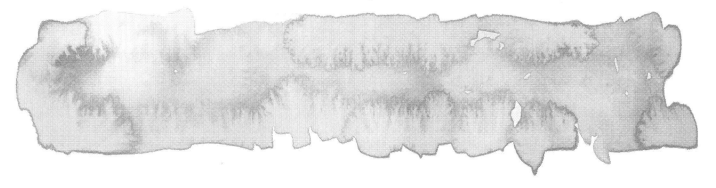

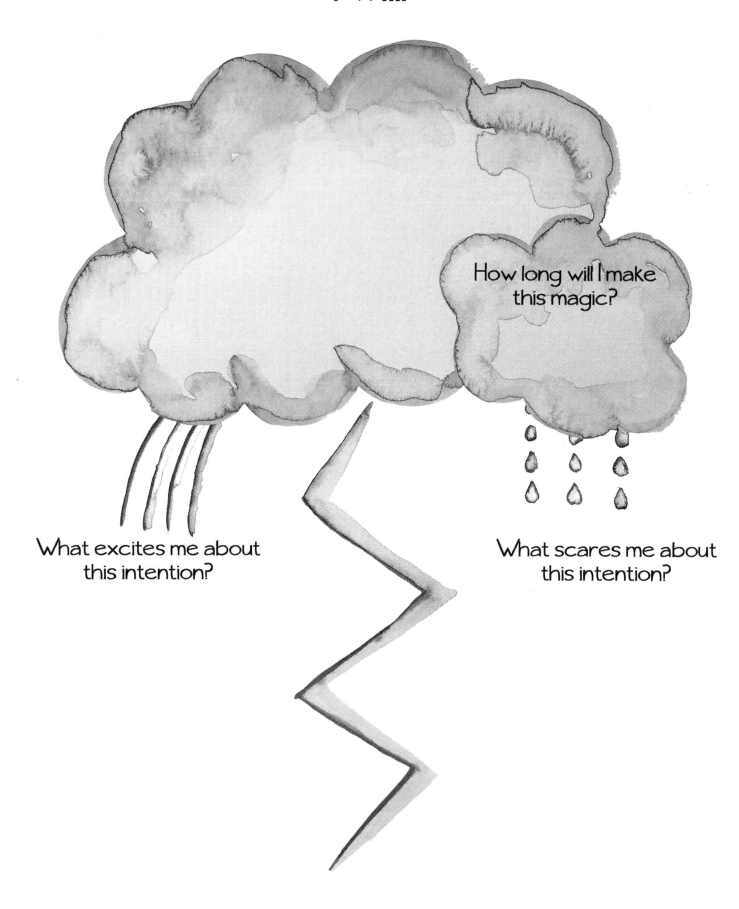

Feel It

Sink into the embodiment of who you will be, what you will feel and what your life will be like when your intention materializes. If you're up for it, write a fable, make a doodle, draw a picture or even just scribble with a color that represents this.

Indulge

Rewrite your intention above.
What can you indulge in that supports your intention?

Reflect

The more you notice the magic that happens, the more it will happen. Use this page to keep track of synchronicities throughout your intention period, write down things for which you're grateful, and reward yourself for loving yourself or taking action. Come back to this page frequently, and watch how the magic unfolds.

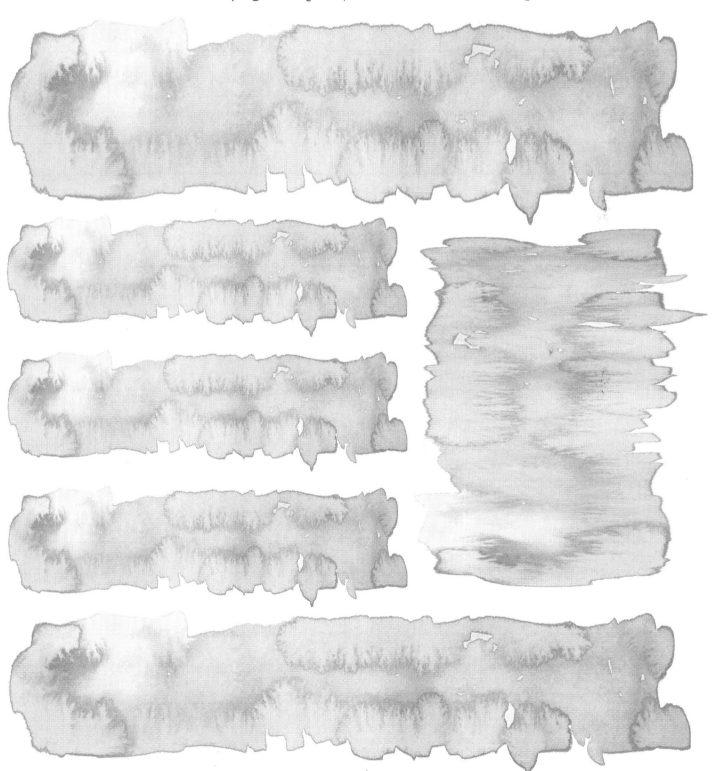

Intention Brainstorm

OK, just start writing. "I intend to..."

STOP. What do I want to bring into my life?

HOLD ON. Breathe. Close your eyes. Picture it. What does your heart desire?

Refine it. Put it all together.

Write it here. My intention is:

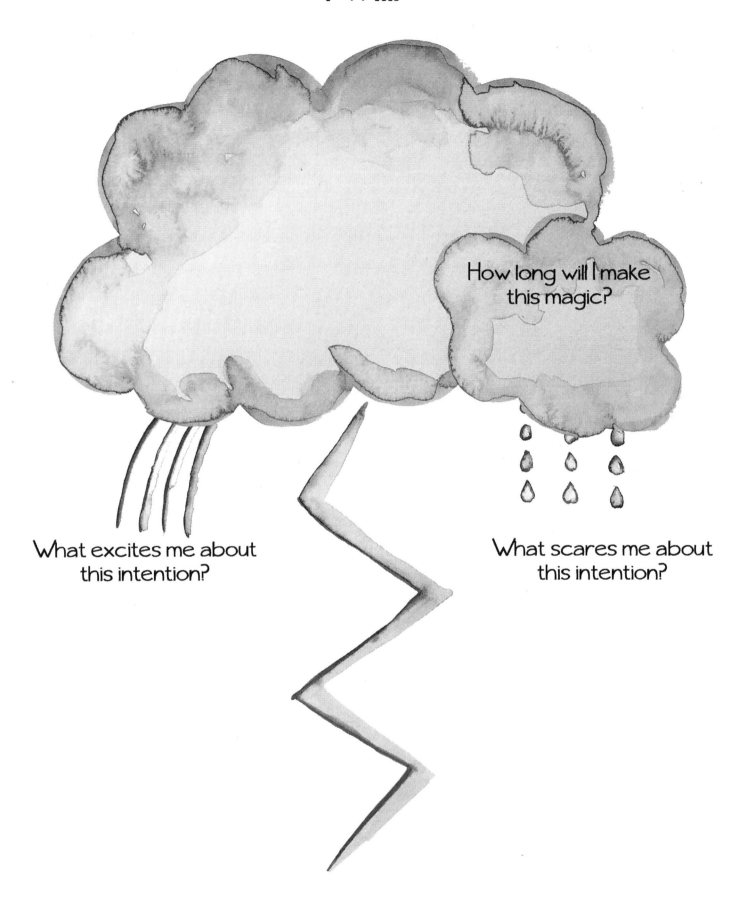

Feel It

Sink into the embodiment of who you will be, what you will feel and what your life will be like when your intention materializes. If you're up for it, write a fable, make a doodle, draw a picture or even just scribble with a color that represents this.

Indulge

Rewrite your intention above.
What can you indulge in that supports your intention?

Reflect

The more you notice the magic that happens, the more it will happen. Use this page to keep track of synchronicities throughout your intention period, write down things for which you're grateful, and reward yourself for loving yourself or taking action. Come back to this page frequently, and watch how the magic unfolds.

Intention Brainstorm

OK, just start writing. "I intend to..."

STOP. What do I want to bring into my life?

HOLD ON. Breathe. Close your eyes. Picture it. What does your heart desire?

Refine it. Put it all together.

Write it here. My intention is:

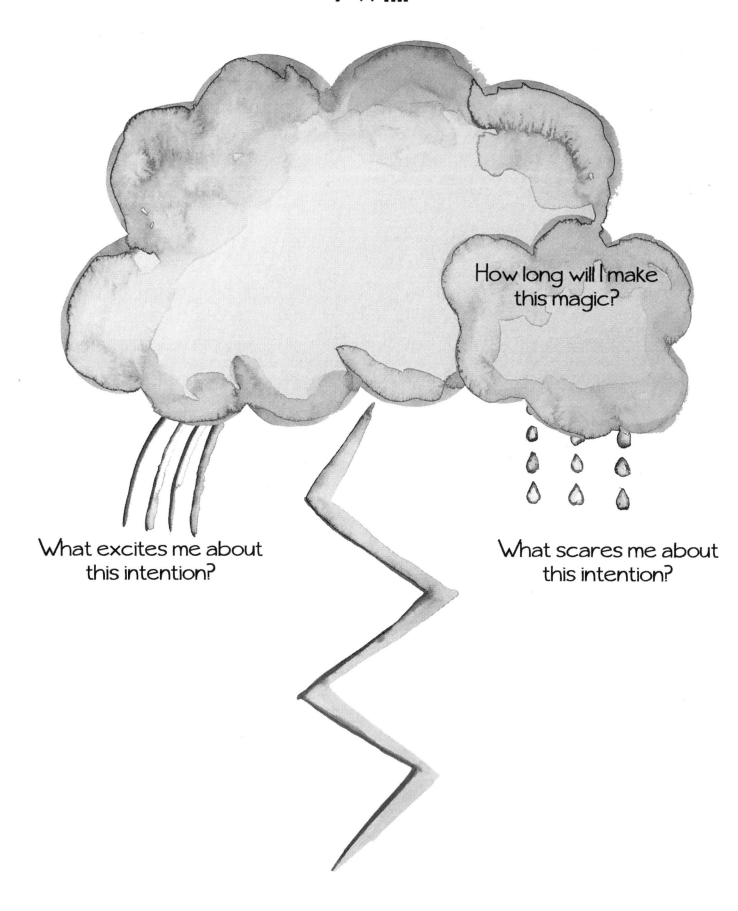

Feel It

Sink into the embodiment of who you will be, what you will feel and what your life will be like when your intention materializes. If you're up for it, write a fable, make a doodle, draw a picture or even just scribble with a color that represents this.

Indulge

Rewrite your intention above.
What can you indulge in that supports your intention?

Reflect

The more you notice the magic that happens, the more it will happen. Use this page to keep track of synchronicities throughout your intention period, write down things for which you're grateful, and reward yourself for loving yourself or taking action. Come back to this page frequently, and watch how the magic unfolds.

Intention Brainstorm

OK, just start writing. "I intend to..."

STOP. What do I want to bring into my life?

HOLD ON. Breathe. Close your eyes. Picture it. What does your heart desire?

Refine it. Put it all together.

Write it here. My intention is:

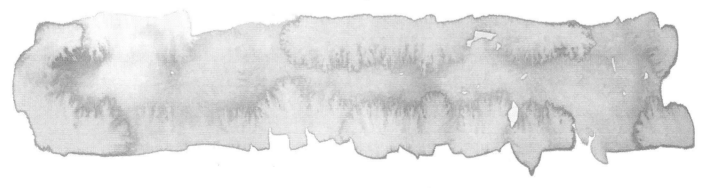

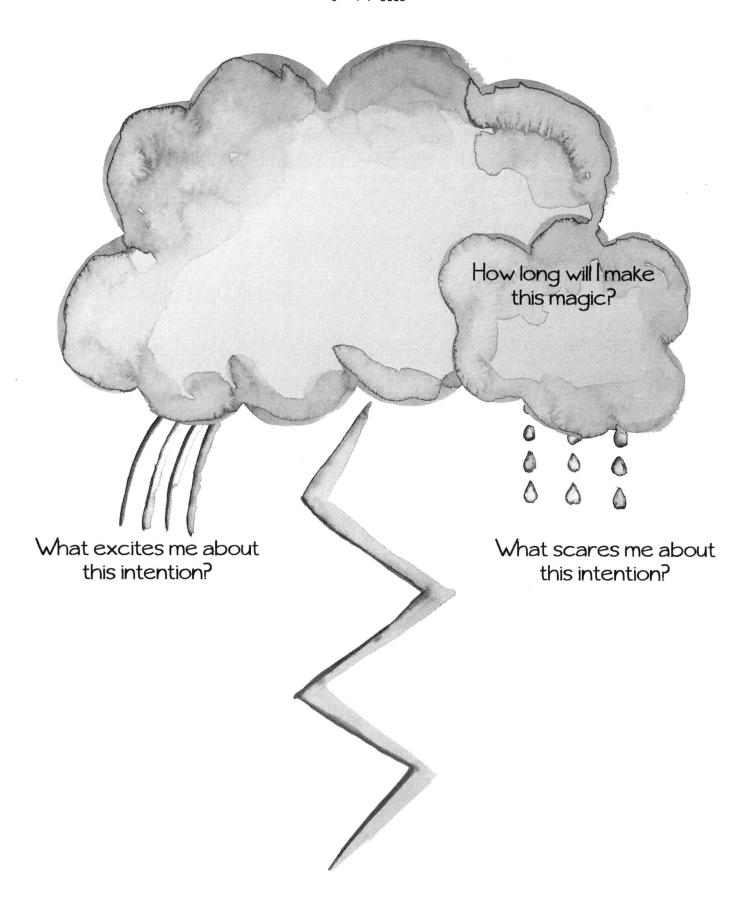

Feel It

Sink into the embodiment of who you will be, what you will feel and what your life will be like when your intention materializes. If you're up for it, write a fable, make a doodle, draw a picture or even just scribble with a color that represents this.

Indulge

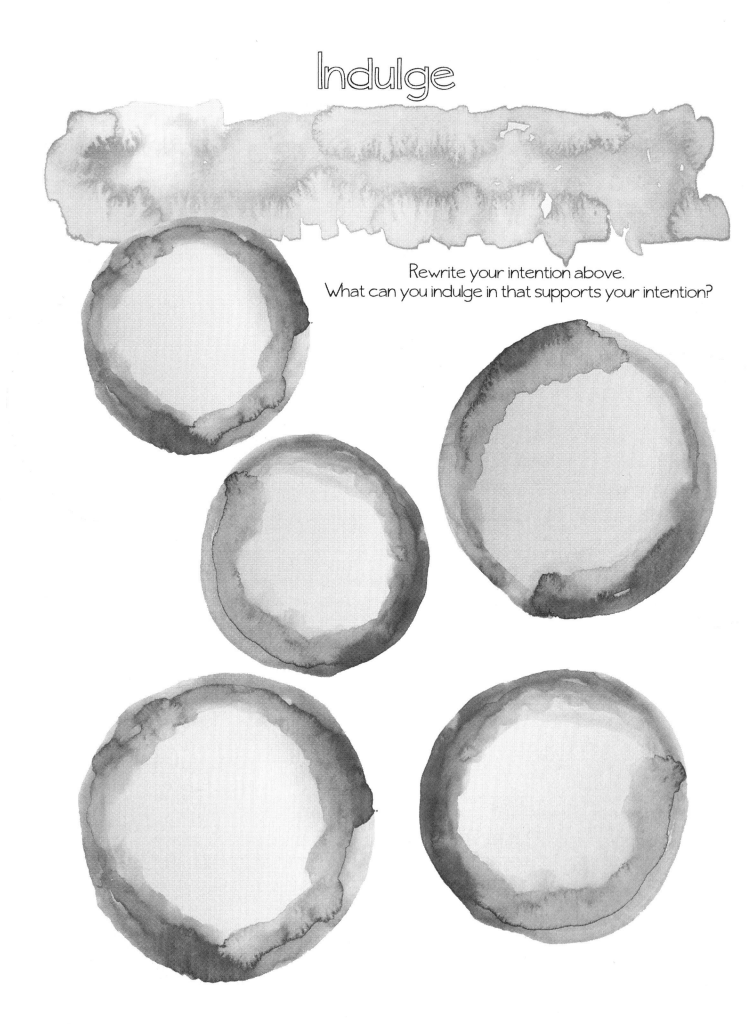

Rewrite your intention above.
What can you indulge in that supports your intention?

Reflect

The more you notice the magic that happens, the more it will happen. Use this page to keep track of synchronicities throughout your intention period, write down things for which you're grateful, and reward yourself for loving yourself or taking action. Come back to this page frequently, and watch how the magic unfolds.

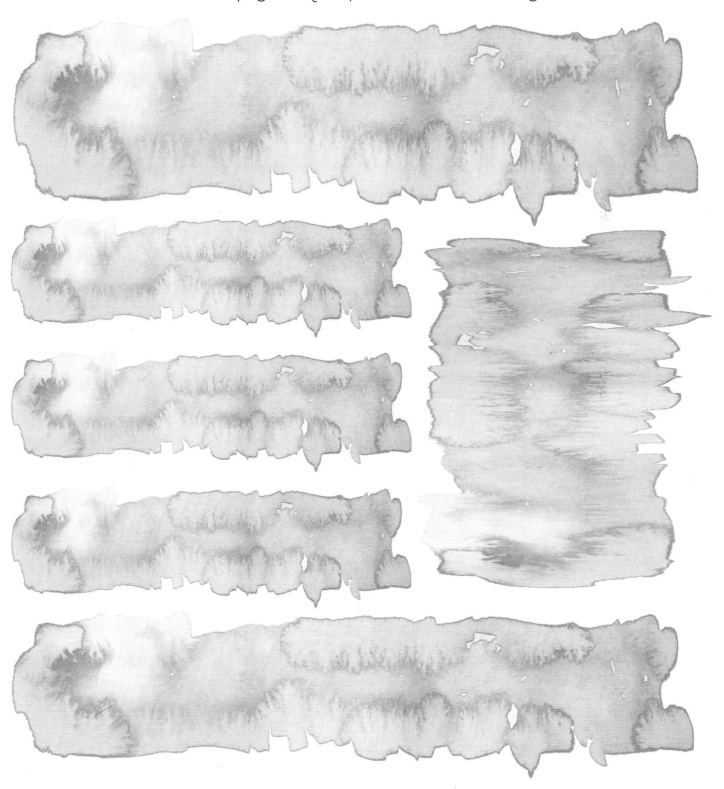

Intention Brainstorm

OK, just start writing. "I intend to..."

STOP. What do I want to bring into my life?

HOLD ON. Breathe. Close your eyes. Picture it. What does your heart desire?

Refine it. Put it all together.

Write it here. My intention is:

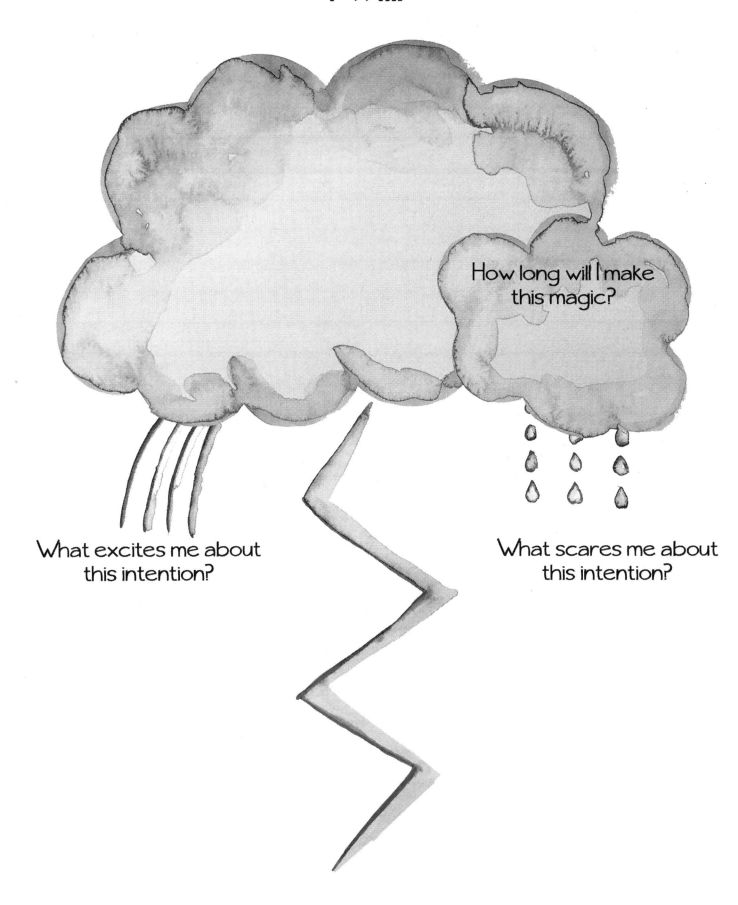

Feel It

Sink into the embodiment of who you will be, what you will feel and what your life will be like when your intention materializes. If you're up for it, write a fable, make a doodle, draw a picture or even just scribble with a color that represents this.

Indulge

Rewrite your intention above.
What can you indulge in that supports your intention?

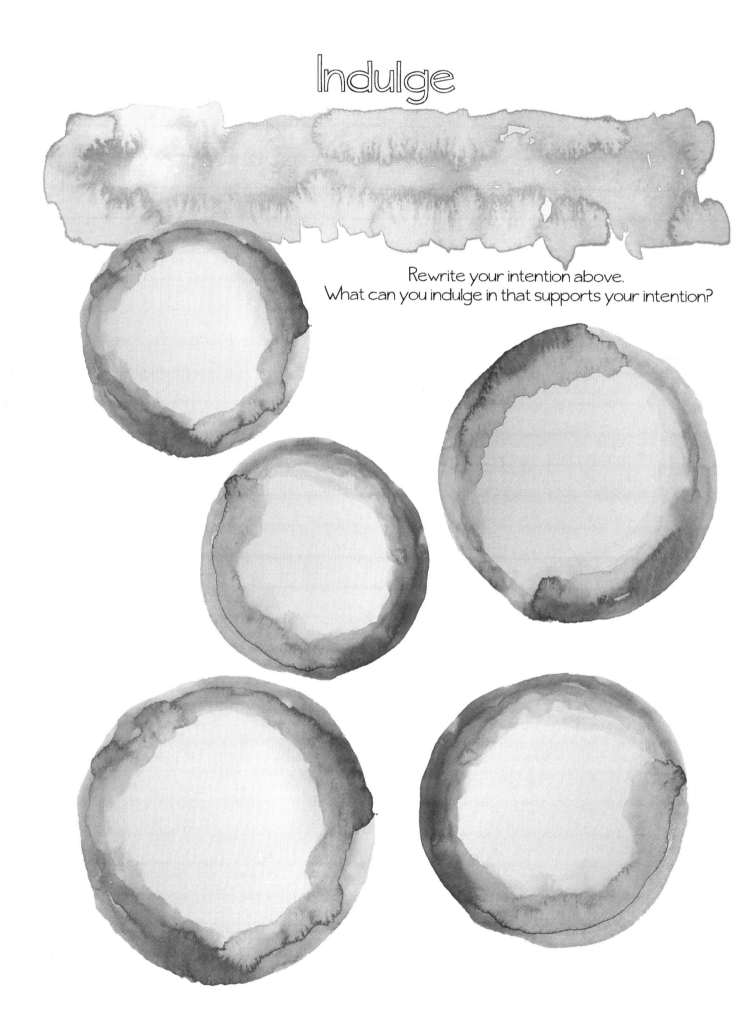

Reflect

The more you notice the magic that happens, the more it will happen. Use this page to keep track of synchronicities throughout your intention period, write down things for which you're grateful, and reward yourself for loving yourself or taking action. Come back to this page frequently, and watch how the magic unfolds.

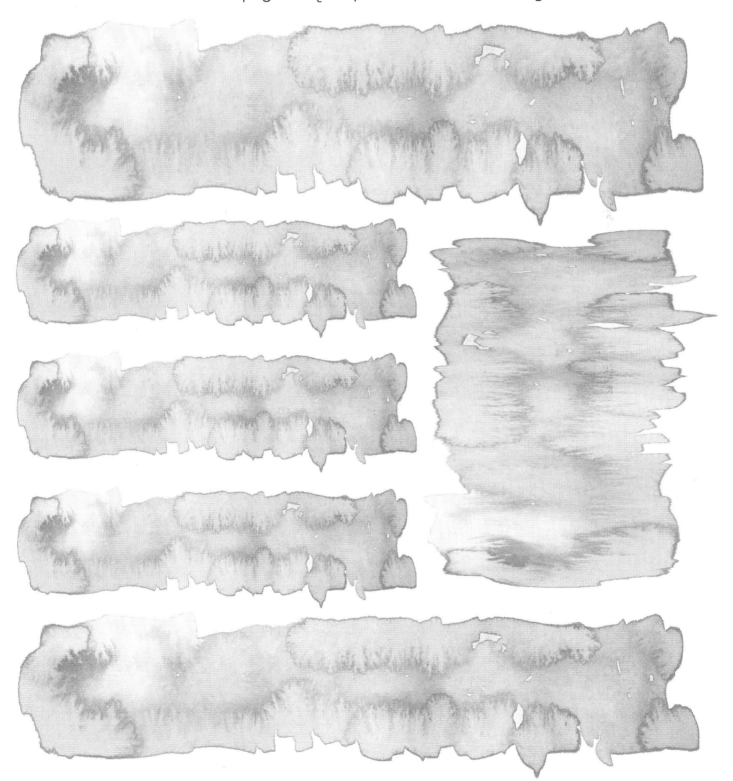

Intention Brainstorm

OK, just start writing. "I intend to..."

STOP. What do I want to bring into my life?

HOLD ON. Breathe. Close your eyes. Picture it. What does your heart desire?

Refine it. Put it all together.

Write it here. My intention is:

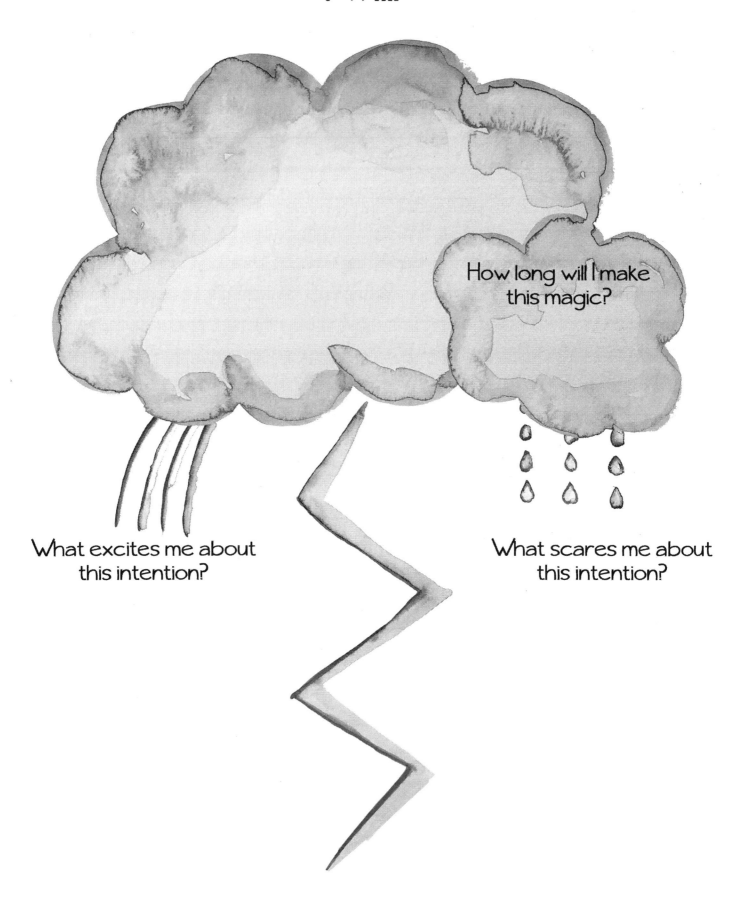

Feel It

Sink into the embodiment of who you will be, what you will feel and what your life will be like when your intention materializes. If you're up for it, write a fable, make a doodle, draw a picture or even just scribble with a color that represents this.

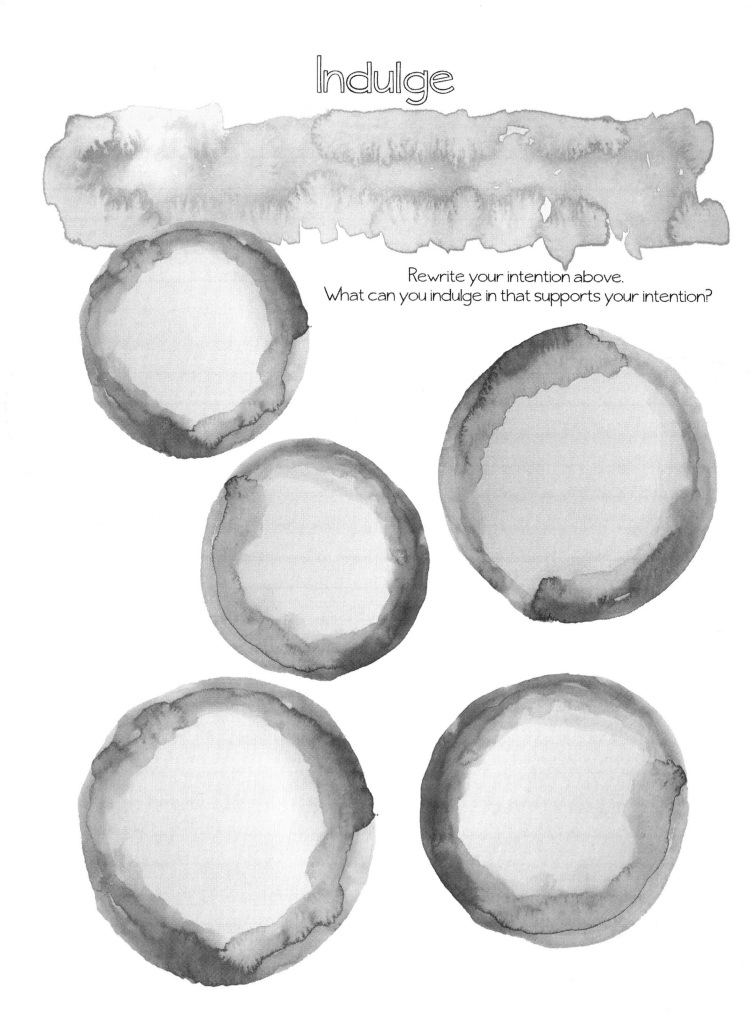

Indulge

Rewrite your intention above.
What can you indulge in that supports your intention?

Reflect

The more you notice the magic that happens, the more it will happen. Use this page to keep track of synchronicities throughout your intention period, write down things for which you're grateful, and reward yourself for loving yourself or taking action. Come back to this page frequently, and watch how the magic unfolds.

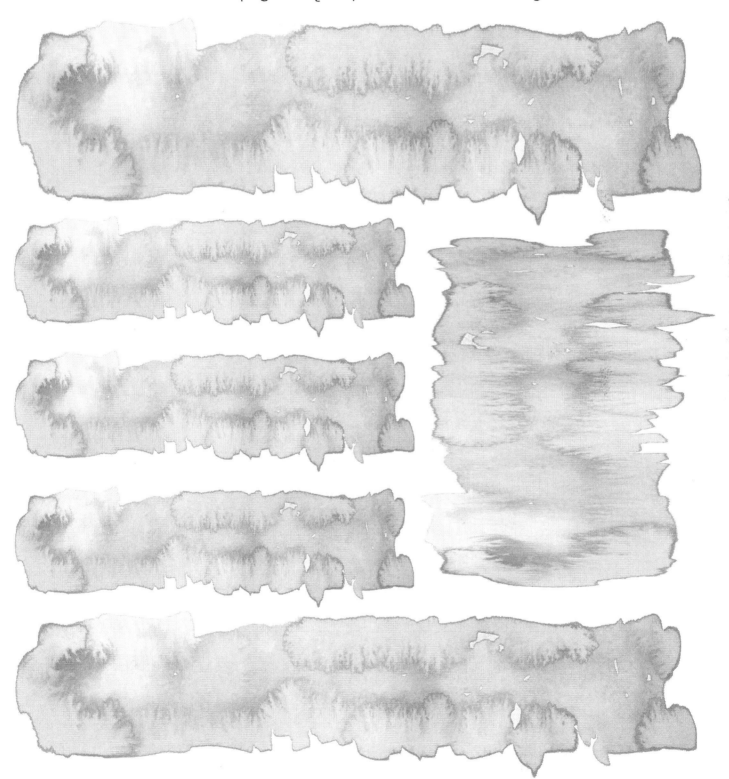

Intention Brainstorm

OK, just start writing. "I intend to..."

STOP. What do I want to bring into my life?

HOLD ON. Breathe. Close your eyes. Picture it. What does your heart desire?

Refine it. Put it all together.

Write it here. My intention is:

I will:

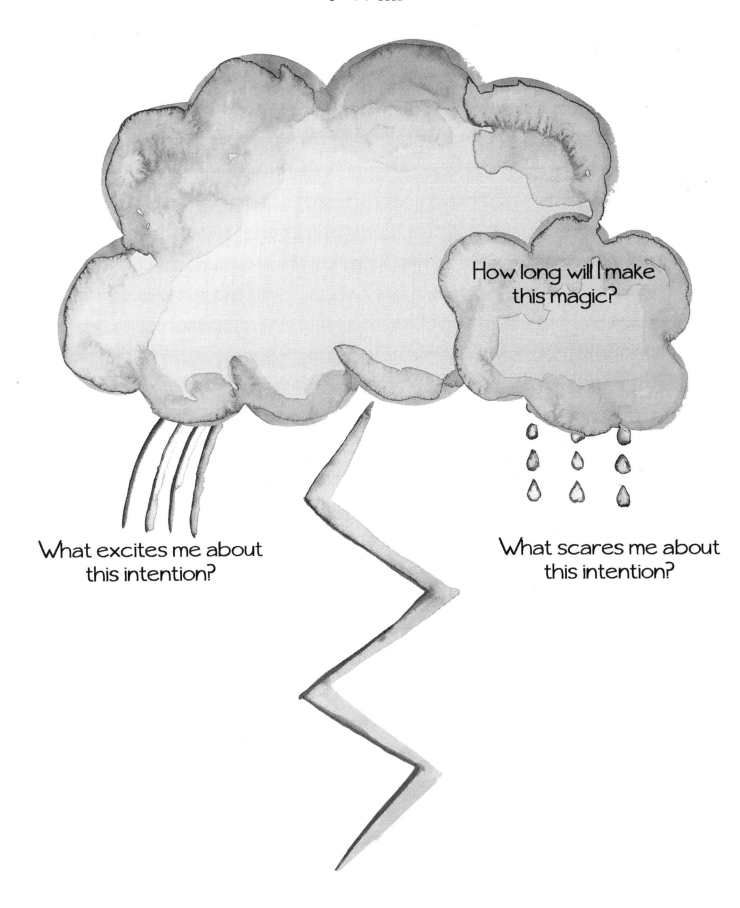

Feel It

Sink into the embodiment of who you will be, what you will feel and what your life will be like when your intention materializes. If you're up for it, write a fable, make a doodle, draw a picture or even just scribble with a color that represents this.

Indulge

Rewrite your intention above.
What can you indulge in that supports your intention?

Reflect

The more you notice the magic that happens, the more it will happen. Use this page to keep track of synchronicities throughout your intention period, write down things for which you're grateful, and reward yourself for loving yourself or taking action. Come back to this page frequently, and watch how the magic unfolds.

Intention Brainstorm

OK, just start writing. "I intend to..."

STOP. What do I want to bring into my life?

HOLD ON. Breathe. Close your eyes. Picture it. What does your heart desire?

Refine it. Put it all together.

Write it here. My intention is:

I will:

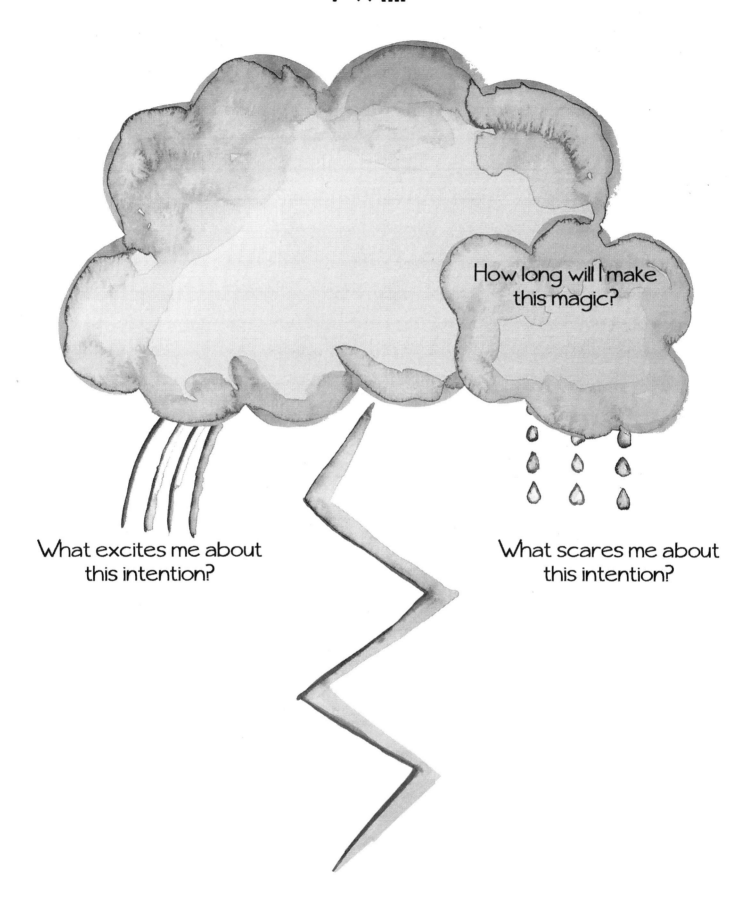

How long will I make this magic?

What excites me about this intention?

What scares me about this intention?

Feel It

Sink into the embodiment of who you will be, what you will feel and what your life will be like when your intention materializes. If you're up for it, write a fable, make a doodle, draw a picture or even just scribble with a color that represents this.

Indulge

Rewrite your intention above.
What can you indulge in that supports your intention?

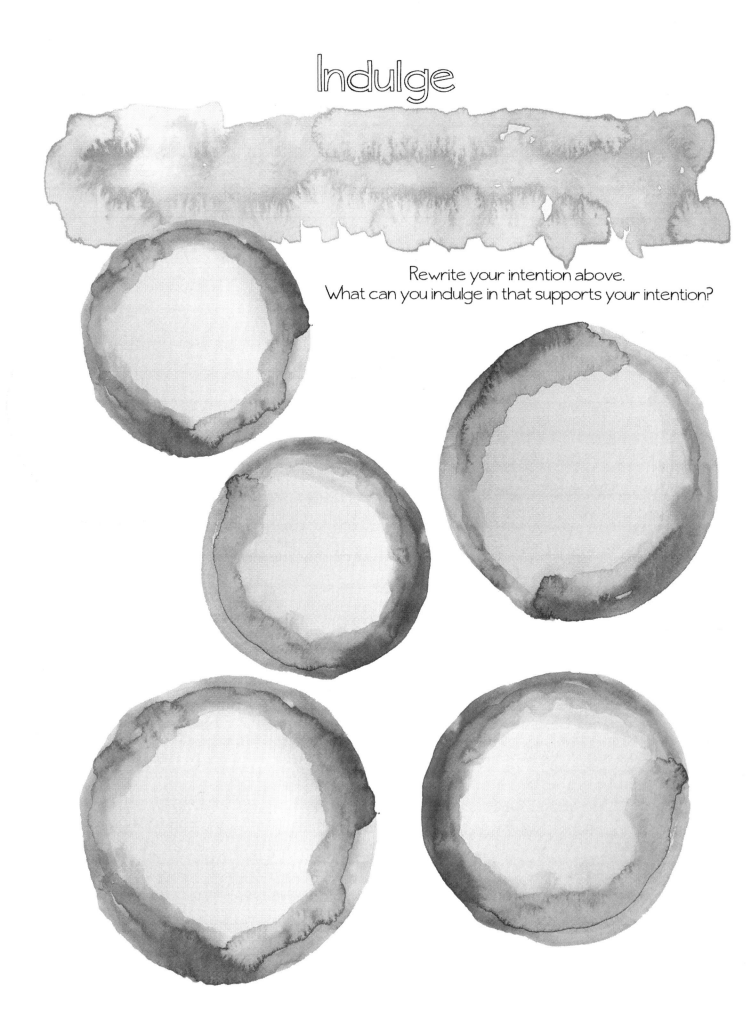

Reflect

The more you notice the magic that happens, the more it will happen. Use this page to keep track of synchronicities throughout your intention period, write down things for which you're grateful, and reward yourself for loving yourself or taking action. Come back to this page frequently, and watch how the magic unfolds.

Intention Brainstorm

OK, just start writing. "I intend to..."

STOP. What do I want to bring into my life?

HOLD ON. Breathe. Close your eyes. Picture it. What does your heart desire?

Refine it. Put it all together.

Write it here. My intention is:

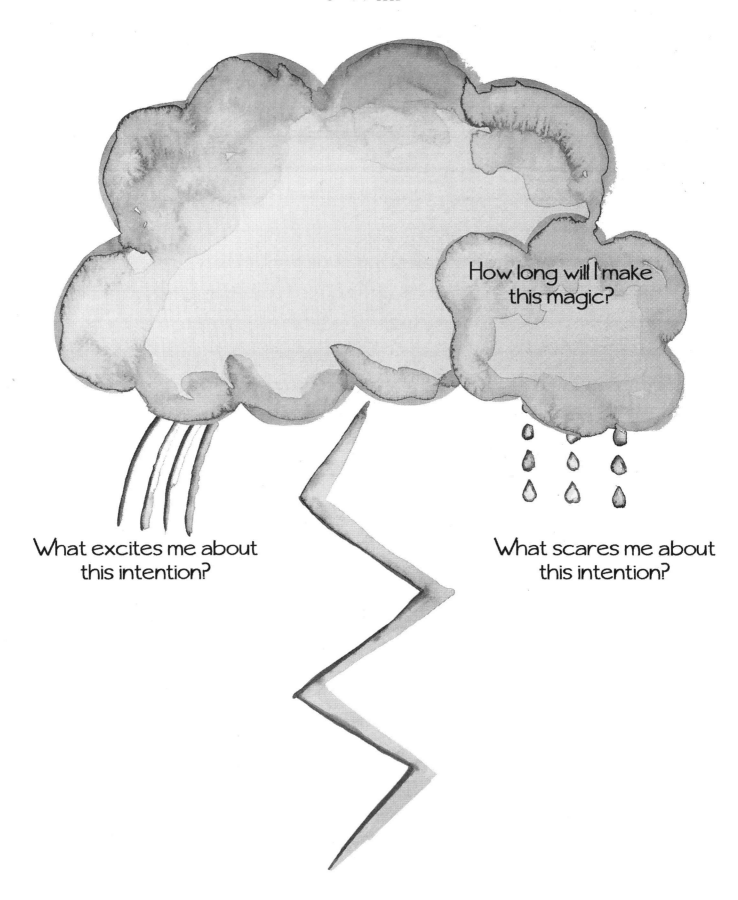

Feel It

Sink into the embodiment of who you will be, what you will feel and what your life will be like when your intention materializes. If you're up for it, write a fable, make a doodle, draw a picture or even just scribble with a color that represents this.

Indulge

Rewrite your intention above.
What can you indulge in that supports your intention?

Reflect

The more you notice the magic that happens, the more it will happen. Use this page to keep track of synchronicities throughout your intention period, write down things for which you're grateful, and reward yourself for loving yourself or taking action. Come back to this page frequently, and watch how the magic unfolds.

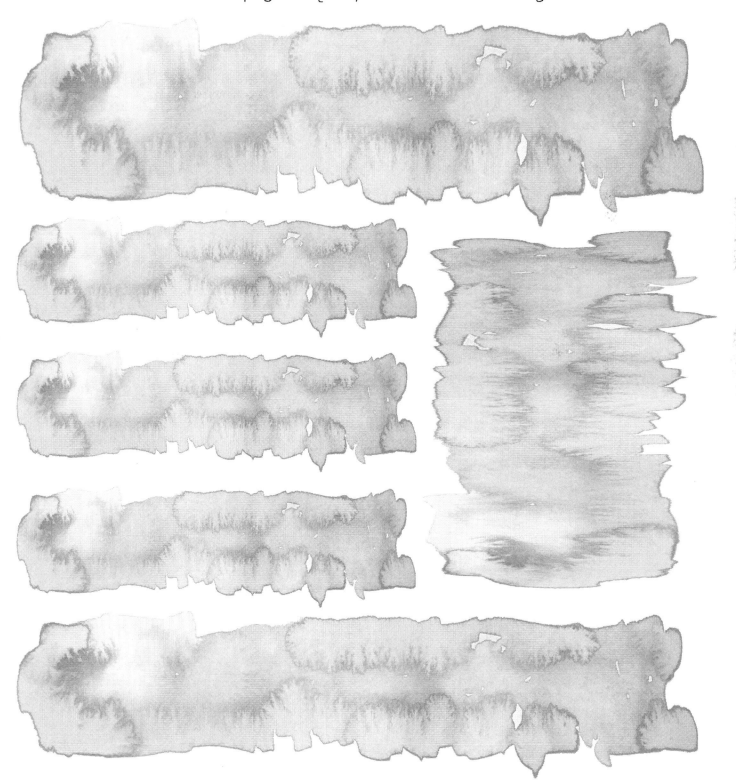

Intention Brainstorm

OK, just start writing. "I intend to..."

STOP. What do I want to bring into my life?

HOLD ON. Breathe. Close your eyes. Picture it. What does your heart desire?

Refine it. Put it all together.

Write it here. My intention is:

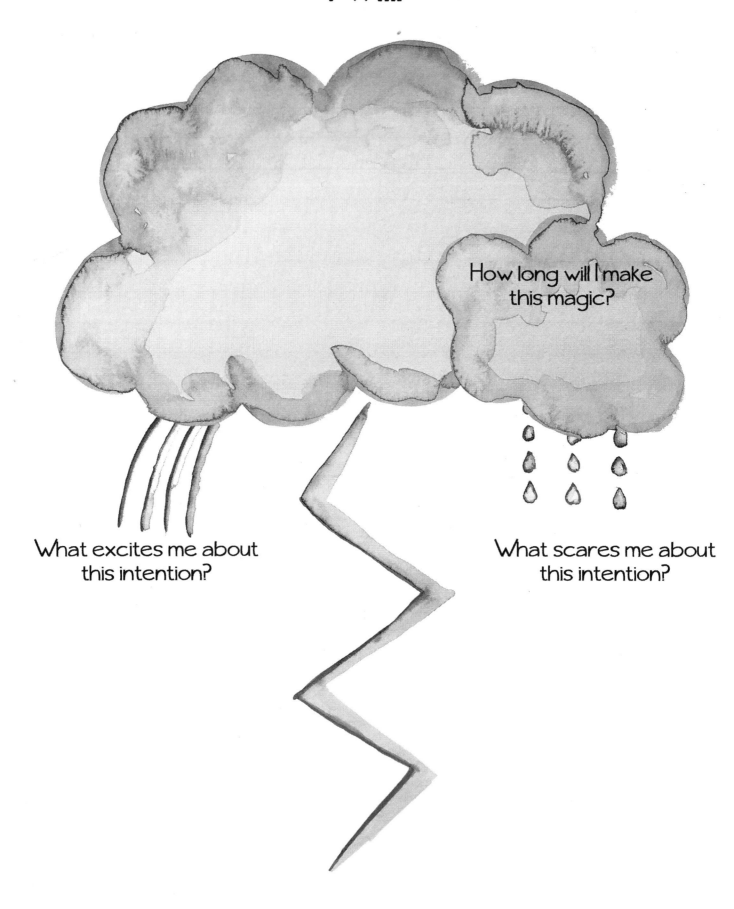

Feel It

Sink into the embodiment of who you will be, what you will feel and what your life will be like when your intention materializes. If you're up for it, write a fable, make a doodle, draw a picture or even just scribble with a color that represents this.

Indulge

Rewrite your intention above.
What can you indulge in that supports your intention?

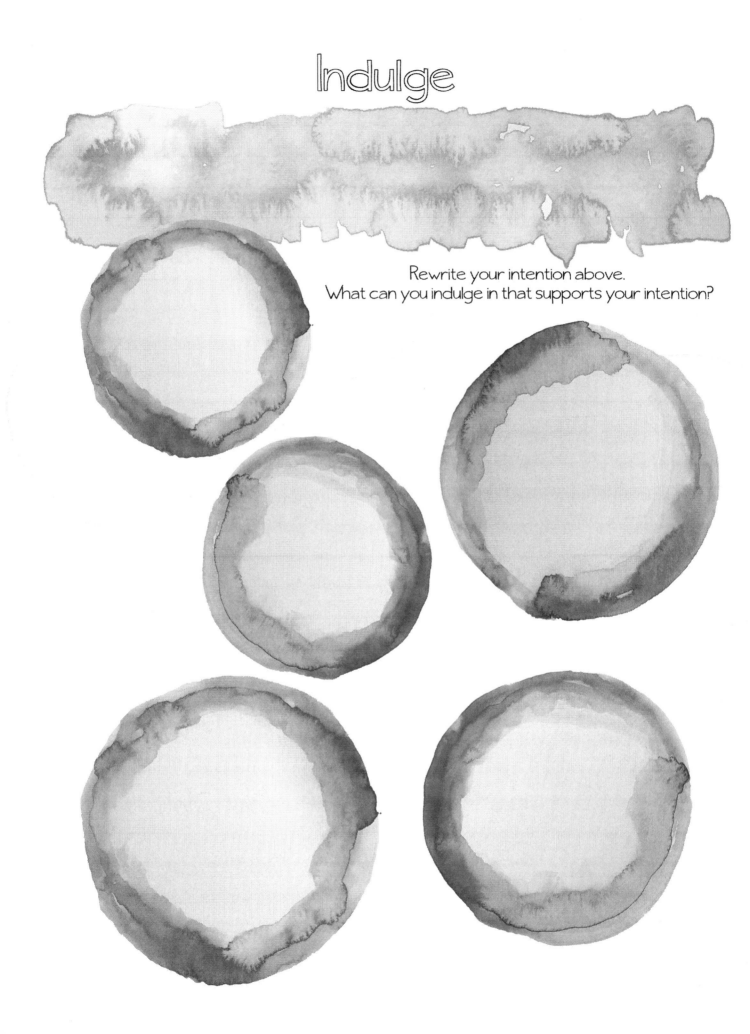

Reflect

The more you notice the magic that happens, the more it will happen. Use this page to keep track of synchronicities throughout your intention period, write down things for which you're grateful, and reward yourself for loving yourself or taking action. Come back to this page frequently, and watch how the magic unfolds.

Made in the USA
Las Vegas, NV
17 October 2022